Poverty

Locating the Author's Main Idea

Poverty

Locating the Author's Main Idea

Curriculum Consultant: JoAnne Buggey, Ph.D.
College of Education, University of Minnesota

By Carol O'Sullivan

Greenhaven Press, Inc.
P.O. Box 289009
San Diego, CA 92198-0009

Titles in the opposing viewpoints juniors series:

Smoking

Gun Control

Animal Rights

AIDS

Alcohol

Immigration

Death Penalty

Drugs and Sports

Toxic Wastes

Patriotism

Working Mothers

Poverty

Library of Congress Cataloging-in-Publication Data

O'Sullivan, Carol, 1945–
    Poverty : locating the author's main idea / by Carol O'Sullivan ;
curriculum consultant, JoAnne Buggey.
      p.   cm. — (Opposing viewpoints juniors)
    ISBN 0-89908-641-1
    1. Poor—United States. 2. Economic assistance, Domestic—United
States.   3. Poverty 4. Hunger. I. Buggey, JoAnne. II. Title.
III. Series.
HC110.P6089 1989
362.5—dc20   89-17069
                                                              CIP

Cover photo: Curt W. Kaldor/UNIPHOTO

CONTENTS

An Introduction to Opposing Viewpoints

When people disagree, it is hard to figure out who is right. You may decide one person is right just because the person is your friend or relative. But this is not a very good reason to agree or disagree with someone. It is better if you try to understand why these people disagree. On what main points do they differ? Read or listen to each person's argument carefully. Separate the facts and opinions that each person presents. Finally, decide which argument best matches what you think. This process, examining an argument without emotion, is part of what critical thinking is all about.

This is not easy. Many things make it hard to understand and form opinions. People's values, ages, and experiences all influence the way they think. This is why learning to read and think critically is an invaluable skill. Opposing Viewpoints Juniors books will help you learn and practice skills to improve your ability to read critically. By reading opposing views on an issue, you will become familiar with methods people use to attempt to convince you that their point of view is right. And you will learn to separate the authors' opinions from the facts they present.

Each Opposing Viewpoints Juniors book focuses on one critical thinking skill that will help you judge the views presented. Some of these skills are telling fact from opinion, recognizing propaganda techniques, and locating and analyzing the main idea. These skills will allow you to examine opposing viewpoints more easily.

Each viewpoint in this book is paraphrased from the original to make it easier to read. The viewpoints are placed in a running debate and are always placed with the pro view first.

Locating the Author's Main Idea

Authors include many ideas in their writing. But each sentence, each paragraph, and even each book they write should contain one main idea. For example, the main idea of this book is that poverty is a much-debated issue.

Locating the author's main idea, whether it is within the sentence, paragraph, or entire piece of writing, is a basic reading skill. It is important because it allows readers to identify the theme of an author's writing. It also allows readers to understand the main point an author is trying to make about the theme.

In this Opposing Viewpoints Juniors book, you will be asked to analyze specific paragraphs to locate the main idea. Sometimes the main idea is placed at the beginning of the paragraph. Sometimes it is placed somewhere within the paragraph or even at the end. For example:

> People have destroyed the homes of many animals by cutting down trees in the rain forest to use for construction. They have also cut short the food supply of many grass-eating animals by using prairie land for building homes and businesses. People's use of the land is threatening the existence of many animals.

The main idea of this paragraph is placed at the end. It is that people's use of the land is threatening the existence of many animals.

When you begin reading the paragraph, you might think the first sentence is the main idea. If it is, then the other sentences in the paragraph will support it in some way. They might explain the idea more specifically or give examples or reasons.

Read sentence two. Does it do any of these things? No. In fact, sentence two is very much like sentence one. Sentence two even says *also,* which suggests that the two sentences are giving two ideas about the same topic.

Now read the last sentence. It is a general statement about the topic of destroying animals' habitats, while the first two are specific examples of this. The last sentence in this paragraph is the topic sentence. The other two sentences support this last sentence.

If you outlined this paragraph, it would look like this:

1. People's use of the land is threatening the existence of many animals.

    A. (Example 1) People have destroyed the homes of many animals by cutting down trees in the rain forest to use for construction.

    B. (Example 2) They have also cut short the food supply of many grass-eating animals by using prairie land for building homes and businesses.

Most paragraphs can be outlined in this way. By reading a paragraph carefully, you should be able to tell which sentence presents the main idea and which sentences explain or support it in some way. Outlining the paragraph may help you figure this out.

We asked two students to write one paragraph each in which they state their main ideas about poverty. Examine the following viewpoints to locate the main ideas.

I think the government should help poor people

The government should help poor people. It should at least give these people decent food. I went downtown with my dad last weekend and I saw people begging for food and money on the streets. That shouldn't be happening in America. A lot of these people would work if they could find jobs. But there just aren't that many jobs available. The government is supposed to help citizens of this country. Poor citizens especially need help.

I don't think the government should help poor people

Helping poor people just makes them stop trying to help themselves. My dad says poor people could find work if they wanted to. But they don't want to because the government pays them with welfare checks when they aren't working. People who don't work get lazier and lazier. Then they start thinking they're worthless and lose their self-respect. The government just hurts poor people, it doesn't help them.

ANALYZING THE
SAMPLE VIEWPOINTS

Kelly and John have very different opinions about whether the government should help poor people. Each presents one main idea in his or her viewpoint.

Kelly:

MAIN IDEA

The government should help poor people.

John:

MAIN IDEA

The government just hurts poor people, it doesn't help them.

Kelly's main idea comes at the beginning of her statement, while John's comes at the end.

As you continue to read through the viewpoints in this book, remember to look for the main idea of the specified paragraphs.

CHAPTER 1

PREFACE: Is Poverty a Serious Problem in America?

America does not have the widespread poverty found in many nations, such as Mexico or India, for example. In fact, since the end of World War II in 1945, America has experienced great prosperity. Because of this, many people believe there is no real poverty in America. To these people, poverty means having only a bowl of rice a day to eat and dying young of a hunger-related illness. It also means having no income, no home, and no hope for anything better.

Other people, however, define poverty differently. They believe poverty means living without things that would be considered luxuries in many countries. These include indoor plumbing, healthy meals every day, and adequate health care. These people argue that not all Americans have these things, therefore poverty does exist in America.

The debate over whether Americans live in real poverty, then, centers around each person's definition of poverty. To some people, poverty means living without many of life's luxuries. To others, poverty means having none of life's luxuries as well as very few of life's necessities, such as food.

The following viewpoints offer differing opinions on the seriousness of poverty in America. As you read these viewpoints, you will be asked to locate the authors' main ideas in specified paragraphs.

VIEWPOINT 1 Poverty in America is a serious problem

Editor's Note: This viewpoint is paraphrased from an article by Allan Sheahen, a businessman and writer. In this viewpoint, Mr. Sheahen discusses the seriousness of poverty in America.

The author's main idea comes at the beginning of this paragraph.

There are many ideas in this paragraph. Transportation, good grooming, and alertness are discussed. But which sentence states the main point that is supported by all these ideas?

What is the author's main idea in this paragraph?

Poverty is America's national disgrace. In this land of plenty, over thirty million Americans live below the poverty level. This means that about 14 percent of the population, or one American in every seven, lives in poverty.

Despite government efforts to help poor people, the situation is getting worse, especially for people sixty-five years old and older. Most of these people are retired and living on fixed incomes. These incomes never increase; however, the cost of living does increase. The result is that many of these elderly people become poorer and poorer. Their retirement incomes are not enough to allow them to purchase the necessities of life.

Another reason for the increase in the number of poor people is inflation. The cost of living is rising faster than people's salaries. Even people who work full time often do not make enough to rise above the poverty level.

It is hard for people to find their way out of poverty once they are in it. In order to look for work, people need transportation. But poor people cannot afford it. And in order to get a job, people have to be well-groomed and neatly dressed. But poor people have no money to buy nice clothes. Also, in order to get a job, people have to look alert and ready to work. People cannot look alert and ready if they have not had a nourishing meal and a good night's sleep on a decent bed.

Even when people can afford the clothes and transportation to look for jobs, there just are not that many jobs available to them. Most of these poor people are unskilled workers. But many jobs require a college degree or knowledge of a trade.

One reporter analyzed all the jobs advertised in a newspaper in Washington, D.C. on one day. That day, there were 1,059 jobs listed. But on the same day, there were 77,600 people looking for jobs in the Washington area. Many of the people were unskilled. After analyzing the jobs, the reporter found that only 256 jobs remained that could be performed by unskilled workers.

There are two main reasons why there are so few jobs available to unskilled workers. First, more unskilled women have joined the work force than ever before. Second, automation and technology are replacing thousands of workers every year. Robots are now performing many of the jobs unskilled people used to perform, at a fraction of the cost. Therefore, there are even more people looking for these jobs.

It seems impossible that in a country as rich as America, people live in poverty. But even though America is a wealthy country, most of that wealth belongs to a few people. The richest 20 percent of the people own 75 percent of all the assets (cars, homes, furniture, and businesses). The poorest 20 percent own no assets at all. And every year, rich people get richer, and poor people get poorer.

Which sentence best expresses the author's main idea in this paragraph?

Read this paragraph carefully. Which sentence best expresses the author's main idea?

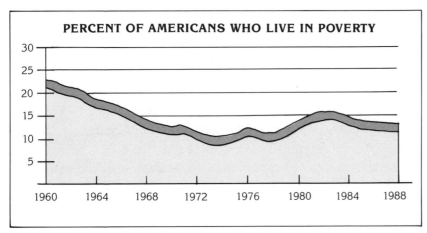

PERCENT OF AMERICANS WHO LIVE IN POVERTY

SOURCE: U.S. Census Bureau

Is poverty a serious problem in America?

How does Mr. Sheahen define poverty? Why does he think poverty is getting worse in America?

What are the two reasons Mr. Sheahen gives to explain why so few jobs are available to unskilled workers?

Can you think of any industries in which automation or technology have taken jobs away from people? Give some examples.

Poverty in America is not a serious problem

Editor's Note: This viewpoint is paraphrased from an article by Bud Shuster, a congressman from Pennsylvania. In this viewpoint, Mr. Shuster expresses his opinion that Americans who live in poverty are much better off than most people in the rest of the world.

Poverty is not a serious problem in America. Americans live better than any other people in the world.

For many people in the world, shivering while starting a fire and running to an outdoor bathroom are everyday experiences. But most Americans know such experiences only from stories of early pioneer days.

Almost every American home now has indoor plumbing, central heating, and electricity. Most homes being built today have two bathrooms, three bedrooms, a fireplace, and a garage. Many have central air conditioning. Nearly all American homes contain all the necessities and many of the conveniences of modern living.

Compared with homes in other countries, most American homes are far more comfortable. Almost half the homes in India have only one room. Almost all are without indoor plumbing. Even in prosperous Japan, the average house has only four rooms and no central heating. Oil-rich Kuwait in Arabia, with the world's highest income per person, has only three-and-one-half rooms per housing unit. Eighty-two percent of them are without running water.

American homes are filled with appliances unavailable in many parts of the world. And in countries where these appliances are available, they cost more than they do in America. For example, an electric or gas oven, refrigerator, washing machine, color TV, vacuum cleaner, and electric iron altogether cost about 2,500 dollars in America. These same items cost 3,200 dollars in Western Europe and 5,200 dollars in the Middle East.

The author's main idea in this paragraph is that nearly all American homes contain the necessities and many of the conveniences of modern living. Do the rest of the sentences in this paragraph support this main idea? Why or why not?

The main idea of this entire viewpoint is that poverty is not a serious problem in America. Does the information in this paragraph support this main idea? Why or why not?

By permission of Johnny Hart and Creators Syndicate, Inc.

Americans also own more cars than other people in the world. Over 114 million cars are registered in the United States. That represents one car for every two people. America has three times as many cars per person as Japan, twice as many as Britain, and twenty times as many as the Soviet Union.

In addition, Americans have more food than people in other countries have. Americans have available the most nutritious, balanced, tasty, and varied diet at the lowest cost. Even high-priced foods in America are bargains compared to their cost in other countries. For example, two pounds of medium-quality steak cost about seven dollars in America, compared to twenty-four dollars in Europe and forty-one dollars in Japan.

Even poverty-stricken Americans live better than many people throughout the world. Most live in one- or two-bedroom homes with a bathroom, a complete kitchen, and modern plumbing. Many poor people own a television set, a radio, and a car. They have adequate clothing. Free health care in modern medical facilities is provided by the government. Food stamps and free school lunches provide balanced diets.

It is true that some Americans may have less than others. But Americans do not live in real poverty. Real poverty means living in total despair. It means existing rather than living, waiting only to die. It means going to bed hungry every night and dying at an early age of a hunger-related disease. Nearly a billion people in the world do live in real poverty. For them, poverty American-style would seem like a luxury. And for these poor billion, poverty means there is no hope of ever being anything but poor.

But this is not true in America. Anyone who is willing to work hard can find a way out of poverty. The American dream is meant to be shared by all.

What is the author's main idea in this paragraph?

Which sentence best expresses the author's main idea in this paragraph?

Which sentence best expresses the author's main idea in this paragraph?

Are any Americans really poor?

How does Mr. Shuster define poverty? Do you agree or disagree? Why?

After reading the previous two viewpoints, how do you define poverty? Do you think poverty exists in America? Why or why not?

Locating the Author's Main Idea

The following paragraphs are based on the viewpoints in this book. Each paragraph contains one main idea. Below each paragraph are two sentences. Circle the one that best expresses the main idea. Remember to read the paragraphs carefully. Many sentences may be related to the main idea, but you must choose the one that *best* expresses the main idea. You may wish to outline these paragraphs before you choose your answer.

EXAMPLE: Many children suffer from poverty. Their parents do not have enough money to buy nourishing food, so the children often go hungry. Also, their parents do not have enough money to buy them warm clothes, so many poor children cannot go to school.

a) The government should help poor children.
b) Many children suffer from poverty.
c) Poor children do not get enough to eat.

The answer is b)—Many children suffer from poverty. This sentence tells us the main idea the author is discussing. Sentence a) is not discussed in the paragraph. Sentence c) supports the main idea.

1. Poor people often have problems finding jobs. They do not have the education or the skills required to do many jobs. Nor do they have the money or clothing necessary to go out and look for a job.

   a) Poor people are usually late for work.
   b) Poor people do not have the education or skill to do some jobs.
   c) Finding jobs can be a problem for poor people.

2. Most Americans have everything they need. There is no real poverty in America. Almost all Americans have indoor plumbing and stoves to cook on. And most American homes, including homes of poor people, have television sets and telephones.

   a) There is no real poverty in America.
   b) Americans have stoves to cook on.
   c) Americans watch too much television.

2

PREFACE: Did the War on Poverty Help the Poor?

During the 1930s, America suffered a Great Depression. This depression was the most severe economic crisis in America's history. During the Great Depression, millions of Americans could not find work. They lost their homes and their life's savings. They became poor.

Before the Great Depression, the government had no full-scale program to help the poor. But with so many people out of work, the government started a program to help America's poor people. President Franklin Roosevelt began a program called the New Deal. This program employed millions of people and provided food for the hungry.

After World War II, America began to recover from the depression. During the 1950s, many Americans earned enough money to buy luxuries such as televisions as well as necessities such as food and shelter. But many Americans were still poor. In 1960, 18 percent of Americans still lived in poverty. In 1964, President Lyndon Johnson began a "War on Poverty." He wanted to help poor Americans have better lives. Similar to President Roosevelt's New Deal, the War on Poverty established programs to help America's needy. Many of these programs are still in use today. For example, Medicaid and Medicare provide medical care to the poor and elderly. The food stamp program helps feed the hungry.

Many people argue that the programs started during Johnson's War on Poverty have helped the poor raise their standard of living. Other people argue that these programs have damaged the self-respect of poor people. They say that when people are given things, such as food and money, they begin to feel helpless. The more helpless they feel, the more helpless they become.

The following viewpoints debate whether the War on Poverty has helped the poor.

Editor's Note: This viewpoint is paraphrased from an article by John E. Schwarz, a professor at the University of Arizona. In this viewpoint, Mr. Schwarz discusses his belief that the War on Poverty reduced the number of people living in poverty in America.

Add up all the people living in Massachusetts, Michigan, Minnesota, Colorado, Oregon, Arizona, Maryland, Kentucky, Iowa, New Hampshire, and South Carolina. This number approximately equals the number of people who lived in poverty in America in 1960.

For many of these people, unemployment was the not the cause of their poverty. In 1960, the heads of about half the families living in poverty held at least part-time jobs. In addition, about one in four heads of impoverished families had full-time employment all year long. Even full-time employment, however, did not provide enough money to keep these families out of poverty.

© 1987 Boston Globe. Reprinted by permission of Los Angeles Times Syndicate.

Realizing that poverty is not always the fault of the poor, in the 1960s, the U.S. government waged a War on Poverty. This War on Poverty included many programs that helped the poor. In 1960, before these government programs, 18 percent of the American people were poor. In the second half of the 1970s, only 4 to 8 percent of the American people lived in poverty. In the space of one generation, poverty had been reduced by 60 percent.

One reason for the decline in poverty during these years was that the nation as a whole was more wealthy. Americans were making more money than ever before.

But this is not the most important reason for the decline in poverty. The main reason poverty declined was that the government stepped in to help poor people. By giving poor people money through food stamps and other assistance programs, the government reduced the poverty level of more than one of every two poor Americans.

By assisting poor people, the War on Poverty raised the quality of their lives. It has provided poor people with basic needs. For example, the food stamp program has provided food to needy people. Dr. Gordon Harper is familiar with the food stamp program. He said that food stamps have helped decrease malnutrition among poor Americans.

Medical programs have also helped many poor Americans. In 1963, before the Medicare and Medicaid programs, 19 percent of poor Americans had never been examined by a doctor. By 1970, only 8 percent had not seen a doctor. The government-sponsored medical programs made it possible for more people to receive medical care either free or at low cost.

These medical benefits improved the health of Americans living in poverty. The infant mortality rate, or rate at which babies die at birth or soon after, proves this. From 1965 to 1975, the infant mortality rate among the poor fell by 33 percent. This is largely because pregnant women received better medical care. It is also because babies received medical care at birth.

Which sentence best expresses the author's main idea in this paragraph?

Locate the author's main idea in this paragraph.

The main idea in this paragraph is that the War on Poverty raised the quality of people's lives. Do the other sentences support this idea? Why or why not?

What is the author's main idea in this paragraph? Which sentences support the main idea?

There are many ideas in this paragraph. No one sentence seems to express the main idea. Read the sentences carefully and decide what main point the author is making with this information.

Many people argue that the War on Poverty hurt poor people as well as helped them. They say that because government programs give money and other assistance to poor people, these people no longer want to work. But this is not true. The desire to work is still strong in America. For most people who receive government assistance, this help is only temporary. They use these programs only when they really need them. As soon as they find work, they withdraw from the program.

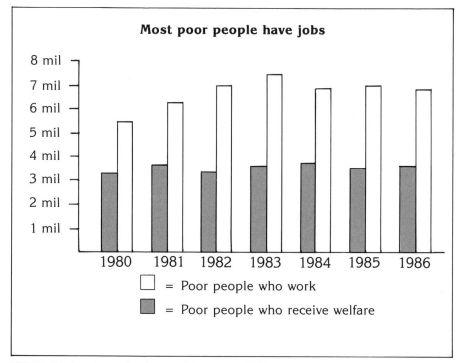

SOURCES: U.S. Census Bureau, Social Security Administration, USN&WR

The quality of life of poor Americans improved much during the War on Poverty. Medical benefits, food and housing, job training, early education for young children, and other programs raised the standard of living for many Americans living in poverty.

Statistics prove that the War on Poverty helped the poor. In 1980, one in fifteen Americans faced poverty, compared with one in five in 1960. This improvement was accomplished almost entirely by government programs.

Which sentence best expresses the author's main idea in this paragraph?

Government help for poor people

What main reason does Mr. Schwarz give for the decline of poverty in the 1960s and 1970s?

Name two basic needs government programs have helped poor people meet.

Editor's Note: This viewpoint is paraphrased from a book by Charles Murray. In this viewpoint, Mr. Murray argues that the War on Poverty hurt poor people.

The social programs begun during the War on Poverty did little to reduce poverty. In 1968, 13 percent of Americans were poor. Fewer people were poor in the 1970s, but by 1980, 13 percent of Americans were again poor.

There is one main reason why the poor did not become any wealthier during the 1960s and 1970s. America as a whole did not do well economically during this time. Inflation, or the rising cost of products, made it difficult for people to buy things. When people cannot buy things, less money circulates. This slows down the economy. Also, many men came home after the war in Vietnam in the 1970s and could not find jobs. When people are unemployed, they have little money to spend. This further contributes to a slow economy. Finally, the cost of energy to heat homes and run automobiles rose in the 1970s. This rise in energy costs meant people had less money to spend on other things.

The main idea in this paragraph is that America suffered economically during the 1960s and 1970s. Do the other sentences support this idea? Why or why not?

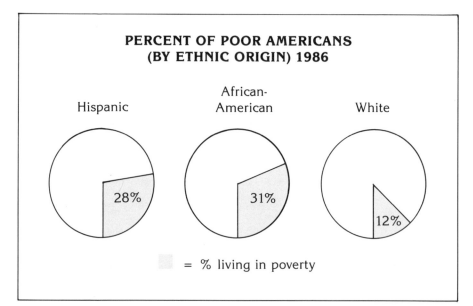

PERCENT OF POOR AMERICANS (BY ETHNIC ORIGIN) 1986

Hispanic — 28%

African-American — 31%

White — 12%

☐ = % living in poverty

SOURCE: U.S. Census Bureau

The government programs begun in the 1960s to help reduce poverty were not enough to help the economy. Thus, poor people remained poor. But the government programs did affect poor people in one way. The programs damaged people's self-respect. By taking away people's responsibility for supporting themselves, the government was saying, "It is not your fault that you cannot do anything to help yourself. America just is not doing well right now." The message people got was that it was no use trying to make a living. They might as well give up.

The author's main idea may be more difficult to locate in this paragraph. Read the paragraph carefully to determine what main point the author is making.

Americans have always believed they could and should work to get ahead. Immigrants arriving penniless in America take any jobs they can and work their way up. Sharecroppers' sons get jobs on assembly lines and work their way out of poverty. These are a few of the personal stories that tell of the ambition and determination of Americans. And America, by providing well-paying jobs, rewards the people who are willing to work.

The government programs begun in the 1960s hurt poor people in another way. Poor people could see that these programs were always made to help the most helpless. They began to feel that if they took part in the programs, they too were helpless. The programs made people who used them feel like failures.

For example, in schools there were special programs for the mentally retarded. There were also programs for the learning-disabled and the emotionally disturbed. Special classes were set up for troublemakers. The purpose was to prevent them from disturbing other students. Every day in typical inner-city schools, young people saw that special programs were directed at troublemakers or people with mental problems. They learned that in order to get a good education, they had to have a problem or cause trouble.

What is the author's main idea in this paragraph? Do the remaining sentences support the author's main idea? Why or why not?

Outside the school, these young people saw that following the rules of society does not always pay off. They saw pimps and drug dealers get rich by breaking the law. They saw people receiving government assistance even though they were healthy and could find jobs. They saw people who had been arrested for committing crimes released into educational programs. These same educational programs were not available to law-abiding poor people.

In addition, when these young people were lucky enough to get a government-sponsored job, they learned that no one really cared whether they worked or not. The people who did not work were treated exactly the same as they were.

These experiences told people that in day-to-day life, there is no evidence that working within the American system pays off. The government programs begun in the 1960s told people one thing: The way to get something from the system was to be a failure or to break the law.

What is the main idea of this entire viewpoint? Does the information contained in this paragraph support this idea? Why or why not?

What government assistance programs did was immoral. They led people to act in ways that destroyed their futures. They made irresponsible citizens out of people who wanted and needed to be responsible. They rewarded people who chose not to work hard rather than hard workers. While trying to help people, government assistance programs have hurt people.

© 1984, Washington Post Writers Group. Reprinted with permission.

We must do something to correct this situation. My advice is to get rid of the entire welfare program. Get rid of unemployment insurance, welfare support, Medicaid, and food stamps. Close down subsidized housing programs. Make people stand on their own two feet. Only then will they realize that they can make it by themselves. Only then will they regain their self-respect. We must cut the knot that ties people to poverty, for there is no way to untie it.

Locate the author's main idea in this paragraph.

How do government assistance programs affect people?

Why does Mr. Murray think government assistance programs damage people's self-respect? Do you agree or disagree? Why?

What does Mr. Murray think school children learned by seeing government-assisted programs in schools? Do you agree or disagree? Why?

CRITICAL
THINKING
SKILL 2 Identifying the Main Idea in
Editorial Cartoons

Throughout this book, you have seen cartoons that illustrate the ideas in the viewpoints. Editorial cartoons are an effective and usually humorous way of presenting an opinion on an issue. Cartoonists sometimes express their main ideas directly. Sometimes they let the readers determine the main idea of the cartoon by observing clues given in the words and illustrations.

Look at the cartoon below. To understand the cartoonist's main idea, you need to know that it would cost the United States government billions of dollars to put a man on Mars. Who are the people in the cartoon? Why are they eating garbage? What main idea is the cartoonist expressing with this cartoon?

For further practice, look at the editorial cartoons in your daily newspaper. Try to decide what main idea the author is expressing in the cartoon.

© 1986 Joel Pett, Lexington Herald-Leader.

CHAPTER

PREFACE: Is Hunger a Serious Problem in America?

In 1967, a team of U.S. senators toured America to evaluate the extent of poverty and hunger. They were distressed by what they saw. Senator George Murphy of California said, "I didn't know that we were going to be dealing with . . . starving people and starving youngsters."

During the 1970s, the government responded to the hunger problem. The food stamp program was expanded so that more poor people could buy food. School lunch and breakfast programs were increased so that more children could get nourishing meals.

In the 1980s, President Ronald Reagan said that hunger was no longer a problem in America. He cut funding for many food programs. The duty of feeding the poor and hungry then fell to private organizations. Churches, soup kitchens, and food banks began providing food to the hungry. Emergency food relief projects were sponsored by corporations and local politicians. And, once again, the hungry were fed.

Some people believe that these private organizations can no longer feed all the hungry. They argue that new reports show that Americans are again starving and that private organizations no longer have the money to feed the poor. What is needed, according to these people, is more government funding for hungry people.

Other people argue that no one is going hungry in America. They say that the new reports contain inaccurate information. They also say the government should spend its money doing more research to find out what the facts about hunger really are. It should not be feeding people who could probably feed themselves.

In the following viewpoints, the authors debate the issue of hunger in America.

Hunger is a national health problem in America. Hunger in America is now more widespread and serious than at any time during the last fifteen years.

Hunger became a national issue in the late 1960s. Social workers reported at that time that many children and elderly people were actually starving. They were suffering from diseases caused by lack of food. And they were dying from these diseases.

Among the poor, child after child suffered from a lack of vitamins and minerals. They were not getting enough milk to drink or fruits and vegetables to eat. They lived on grits and bread. Many had severe eye, ear, and bone diseases. Hunger damaged the health of many children during the 1960s.

Then government programs began providing food to needy families. The food stamp program was expanded. This allowed more poor people to buy food. School lunch and breakfast programs were increased so children could have good nutrition while they learned. Elderly people who were confined to their homes were brought nourishing food to eat. All across the country, new programs were helping people obtain proper nourishment. And ten years later, by the late 1970s, the hunger situation had improved.

Now, hunger is once again a problem in America. Extensive hunger is found in every state. For example, nine-year-old Lee, who resides in rural Missouri, is the size of a six-year-old because he does not get enough to eat. Ninety-two-year-old Laura McAfee, who eats only white beans and potatoes, is thin and suffering from iron deficiency in Nashville. Mr. Alvarez collects cans near Brownsville, Texas, so his wife and granddaughter can eat. And in St. Louis, children dig for food in the dumpsters outside apartment buildings.

Which sentence best expresses the author's main idea in this paragraph?

Locate the author's main idea in this paragraph. Which sentences give additional information about the main idea?

Nearly a half-million children in America are undernourished. Growth failure and low birthweights among children are associated with poor nutrition. And health problems and diseases are common in elderly people who do not get enough to eat. Children and the elderly are most affected by poor nutrition.

No one knows the exact number of hungry Americans. But reports indicate that up to twenty thousand citizens may go hungry for several days each month.

Emergency food programs report large increases in the number of hungry people. Evidence suggests that hunger is continuing to grow. It is true that America's economy has improved. But this improvement has not affected hunger in America. The poor are still poor. And they are hungrier than ever.

People should not be starving in America. Hunger should not happen in a country with more than enough to feed itself and much of the world. Hunger in America is the result of government failure to meet the needs of the people. Government leaders have cut back on programs that help citizens endure hard times. They have cut back on these programs at a time when they are most needed. Poverty is at its highest rate in over twenty years. As a result, America has become a "soup kitchen society." This means that people all over the country are lining up at churches, the Salvation Army, and other organizations for free food.

Our political leaders must recognize the seriousness of hunger in America. They must do something to help the millions of Americans who are hungry. It is their job to make sure that all Americans benefit from the plentiful supply of food in America.

> What is the author's main idea in this paragraph? Do the remaining sentences support this idea? Why or why not?

> What is the main idea of this entire viewpoint? Does this paragraph support this main idea? Why or why not?

Hunger in America

Which two groups of people does the author say are most affected by poor nutrition? What health problems does the author say affect these two groups of people?

What reason does the author give for hunger in America?

Editor's Note: This viewpoint is paraphrased from an article by S. Anna Kondratas. Ms. Kondratas is the head of the Food and Nutrition Service for the U.S. Department of Agriculture. In this viewpoint, Ms. Kondratas criticizes the hunger study paraphrased in Viewpoint 5. She argues that the problem of hunger in America has been exaggerated.

Locate the author's main idea in this paragraph.

The Physician Task Force on Hunger in America (PTFHA) has suggested that millions of Americans are hungry. Some people even claim that there is famine in America.

But there are no facts to prove that millions of Americans are hungry. In fact, in the late 1970s, studies reported that hunger is not a problem in America. The studies indicated that hunger exists in only a few homes across the country.

Since the 1970s, the government has spent a lot of money to help feed the poor. Many programs have been started by the government and private citizens to deal with hunger. More poor people are receiving food stamps than ever before. And more wealthy people are contributing to funds that help feed the poor.

So what would explain rising hunger? Nothing. The truth is that there is no reason to believe the problem is any worse than it was in the late 1970s. In fact, the hunger situation has probably improved.

The author is discussing a particular study done on hunger. What main point is she making about this study?

A study done by the PTFHA titled *Hunger in America* concluded that hunger is a problem in this country. The study found that there are at least twenty million hungry Americans. By hungry, researchers meant that people did not have enough money to buy nourishing food. But this study simply ignored other surveys that had been done on poor people. These surveys said that the majority of poor people had plenty of food.

Which sentence best expresses the author's main idea in this viewpoint? Do the remaining sentences support this idea? Why or why not?

This and other studies that indicate that people are going hungry were done improperly. One way researchers determined whether people were hungry was by looking in their refrigerators to see if they contained food. When the refrigerators were empty, people were said to be hungry. But in many cases the people denied that they were hungry. They just had not had time to buy food.

This kind of research is unprofessional and dishonest. In short, *Hunger in America* is an example of careless research and is unfair to the government programs meant to help the poor. The government spends nearly twenty billion dollars a year on food programs. Yet, the PTFHA claims that its study proves the government has failed to meet the needs of hungry people. The study, however, proves nothing.

The fact that this study fails to prove that Americans are going hungry does not mean government leaders should just forget about hunger. The government should spend money on more surveys to determine once and for all if Americans are going without proper nourishment. This would help decide whether hunger is a problem in America.

What is the main idea of this entire viewpoint? Does this paragraph support this main idea? Why or why not?

Hunger Throughout the World

■ = Hungry nations

☐ = Non-hungry nations

SOURCE: The Hunger Project

Is hunger a problem in America?

What is Ms. Kondratas's criticism of studies that prove the government has failed to meet the needs of the hungry?

After reading viewpoints 5 and 6, do you think hunger is a problem in America? Why or why not?

Below are eight statements. Each is related to the information you have read in these viewpoints. Choose one and make it the main idea of a paragraph you write.

EXAMPLE: Topic Idea: The government has sponsored many programs to help the poor.

The government has sponsored many programs to help the poor. The food stamp program, created in the 1960s, has helped poor people buy food. This program gives poor people stamps to pay for their food. The poor people pay only what they can afford for the stamps. Also during the 1960s, the government created medical programs called Medicaid and Medicare. These programs allow poor people and the elderly to receive medical care free or at a small cost.

Main Ideas:

1. Hunger is a serious problem in America.

2. Poor people have a hard time finding jobs.

3. There are no truly poor people in America.

4. The War on Poverty helped poor people.

5. The government must help feed hungry people.

6. Poor people need to learn to help themselves.

7. Poverty exists in America.

8. Jobs are hard to find in America.